Inspirational and Heart-Felt Rhymes About Our Times

Mertis Hodge Butler

World rights reserved. This book or any portion thereof may not be copied or reproduced in any form or manner whatever, except as provided by law, without the written permission of the publisher, except by a reviewer who may quote brief passages in a review.

The author assumes full responsibility for the accuracy of all facts and quotations as cited in this book. The opinions expressed in this book are the author's personal views and interpretations, and do not necessarily reflect those of the publisher.

This book is provided with the understanding that the publisher is not engaged in giving spiritual, legal, medical, or other professional advice. If authoritative advice is needed, the reader should seek the counsel of a competent professional.

Copyright © 2021 Mertis Hodge Butler
Copyright © 2021 TEACH Services, Inc.
ISBN-13: 978-1-4796-1254-3 (Paperback)
ISBN-13: 978-1-4796-1255-0 (ePub)
Library of Congress Control Number: 2020917054

Scripture quotations marked NKJV are taken from the New King James Version®. Copyright©1982 by Thomas Nelson, Inc. Used by permission. All rights reserved.

Table of Contents

I. Introduction
    Reviews

II. Seeking Peace
    Come with Me
    Look to Jesus
    The Wisdom from Above
    Just Praise God
    Dreams
    The Good Old Days
    A New Year

III. Knowing Who You Are
    We Are Christian Soldiers
    The War of the Ages
    Today's Changing World
    Carnal-Minded/Christian Dilemma

IV. Getting Ready
    Are We Ready for Jesus to Return?
    Ready to Go Home
    The Understanding
    I Am Committed
    This Is My Mission

V. Patriotism
    Where Is the American Dream?
    Heed the Signs I

    The Desirable Switch
    Tax-Paying Poor
    Why?
    Heed the Signs II
    A Change Is Needed
    Lord, Help Us Through

VI. Unique and Special People
    Your Smile
    The Precious Gift
    Thanks, Mom and Dad
    Little Black Boy
    Old Man
    Mentors
    The Brightest Star in the Galaxy
    Girl
    Women of God
    Fashion Analysis
    Body Parts Chitchat

VII. God's Little Creatures
    The Transit Bus Hijack
    The Stalking Squirrel

VIII. Mystifying English
    A Tot's Puzzling Journey
    The Quaint "Q"
    The Transit "T"
    The "T" Trail
    The Unique "U"
    The Zesty "Z"
    Which Tense Makes Sense?

I. Introduction

This collection of poems by Mertis Hodge Butler represents a variety of thoughts and themes from all walks of life. They are the poet's expressions in rhyme about our modern times. The collection embraces religious, political, humorous, and educational themes, mixed with truth, personal feelings, and experiences.

Mertis is a graduate of Tuskegee Institute, Tuskegee, Alabama, and Atlanta University, Atlanta, Georgia. Her major in elementary education is reflected in the inspired way she teaches some of the alphabet in the last section of this book (VIII).

Many of her poems address her study, dedicated work, and service as a woman of God. Her prayer is that this book of poems will motivate, inspire, and encourage all who read them.

She credits her parents, David and Minnie Bell Hodge, and God's Holy Word as the inspiration and main source of her ability to compose. She is very grateful to relatives, friends, co-workers, and Christian brethren who encouraged her to publish her poems.

She is especially thankful to her daughter, Sandra Woolford, who helped to edit the original draft for publishing.

—Mertis H. Butler

Reviews

"A warm blessing will be received by reading this book of poetry by our beloved church member, Mertis Butler. With so much decay and turmoil unfolding within society, just as Christ forewarned us, Sister Butler's poetic reflections in spiritual discernment, wisdom, and humor are encouraging and uplifting. Her love for Jesus and sharing Him with others exudes in her writings. It is our prayer that lives will be touched and turned toward our Lord and Savior, Jesus Christ, as they read this book."

—Pastor Phil and Ellen Roberts

"Sister Mertis, as she is affectionately known by many, is a rare and precious jewel. She is fierce and feisty; she is Spirit-filled and Spirit-led. I am so grateful and inspired that she decided to put a few of her thoughts and experiences into this book of poetry. Utilizing simple yet profound prose, mostly in rhyme, you will be transfixed by the common-sense approach with which she tackles some difficult and important life lessons, societal ills, and some humor thrown in to keep us on our toes.

"One minute you will be cheering her on and the next you will be laughing your head off. Contemplate, meditate, and enjoy. Maybe we can encourage her to pen Volume II. I am inspired by this 82 years young woman of God to be publishing her first book but certainly not her last, and I couldn't be more proud of my mother/friend."

—Jeanette Metts Whetstone, Church Sister and Friend

II. Seeking Peace

Often in life, especially in these modern times, people are searching for something, but know not what. One thing or another is tried without finding the peace they are seeking.

Each poem in this section gives some spiritual inspiration for those who are seeking peace. My prayer is that they give inspiration and hope, based on biblical truths, to all who are confused with various doctrines and alternative truths.

Come with Me

Come and go with me to a special place
where there is only peace and oneness with God.
Come with me and find His amazing grace
in a place where many others have trod.

This place can be in your heart or mind,
on a hill, in your home, or at your desk.
The main ingredient is for you to find
the place where communion with God is best

Look to Jesus

When troubles engulf you
with no end in view,
Look to Jesus Christ.
He knows just what to do.

When there is no hope or peace
in the place where you are,
you can always find release
in Jesus, whether near or far.

The burdens of living each day
are sometimes so hard and unfair.
To be victorious, there's only one way:
staying in Jesus' loving care.

Let Jesus be your focus always.
Keep Him first in everything you do.
Rely on His promises all of your days,
and He will carry you through!

The Wisdom from Above

The wisdom of God, comes from above.
He gives it out of His pure love.
The wisdom of God is real and true.
He is always willing to give it to me and you.

God's wisdom counsels and teaches
and is always helping as He preaches.
To all who will listen and obey,
He will lead and direct in the right way.

Wisdom gives understanding to every man
who read and study God's Word with a plan.
It does not matter who you are.
Wisdom is the one thing that will take you far.

In a world that is so demanding,
"Get Wisdom! Get Understanding!"
This is what Proverbs 4:5 says.
Remember, WISDOM is needed always.

Just Praise God

When things are at their very worst,
    PRAISE GOD!
Give thanks for your sorrows and your woes.
Thank Him for your distresses and your foes.
    JUST PRAISE GOD!

When things are at their very worst,
*   PRAISE GOD!*

Even when you think God has forsaken you,
    PRAISE HIM!
Seek His will and way for all circumstances.
Nothing in life is by luck or mere chances.
    JUST PRAISE HIM!

When all is serene and going well,
    PRAISE GOD!
Praise Him for health and for being alive.
Thank Him for how He's helped you to survive.
    JUST PRAISE GOD!

Dreams

Dreams, dreams, we all have dreams.
Some are vain, and some are like shiny sunbeams.
Dreams burst forth through hardships and trials.
They often help us through the day with a smile.
Some dreams are followed with a fervent will,
until, at last, "The Dream" is fulfilled!

The Good Old Days

Oh how I miss the "good old days"
when minds were serene,
clear, and morally clean.
Most people were not so easily swayed.

Oh, how I miss the "good old days"
when God was always supreme.
People would help others in many ways,
even when their earnings were lean.

Oh, how I miss the "good old days"
when cost for goods were not so high.
Back then, people knew how to really pray.
The common worker could save and retire.

It's true, those days are passed and gone.
The country has departed from "In God We Trust."
Back then, this country was very strong.
I don't want to consider what will happen to us!

A New Year

A new year is here; what is your plan—
to live it for God, or live it for man?
Will your days be wasted with careless demands?
Or will they be scheduled with a daily plan?

Last year has passed; it is forever gone.
There is no need to dread bad memories and mourn.
You now have new opportunities and things to learn;
new friends to make, and new problems to discern.

III. Knowing Who You Are

It is very important to know who you are. The world around us is continuously changing each and every day, and life is short. Having a good biblical foundation is necessary, but not always a reality. Who you are is a total composite of your parents, their backgrounds, and your background; what you are taught, and what you learn as you journey through this changing world.

Always make the best of whatever comes into your life. There is only today, for yesterday is past and gone and tomorrow is not promised.

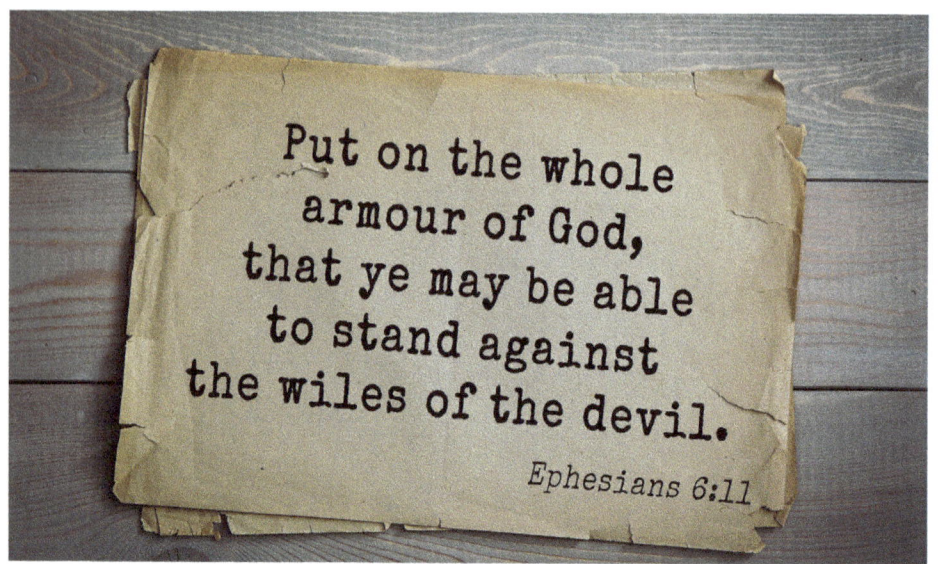

We Are Christian Soldiers

We are soldiers in God's Christian army.
Often, we know not who or what we fight.
Paul in Ephesians six reminds you and me
to fight this darkness with Christ's light.
Paul tells us to put on "the whole armor of God."
With it, against the wiles of the devil, we can stand.
Our head, heart, loins, and feet must be securely shod,
while keeping God's sword and shield in hand.
We must watch and, in the Spirit, always pray.
We stand in the strength supplied alone by God.
We must not look back, only forward, and not stray.
Always having unwavering faith in Jesus, our Lord.
Soldiers, we must be strong in truth and righteousness,
carrying with us always the gospel of peace.
Knowing the salvation Jesus provided is our sure success,
as long as His word is in our hearts, and never cease.
Soldiers of Christ, now is the time to arise.
Christian soldiers, let us put all our armor on.
Let us stand strong in the strength, which God supplies
through Jesus Christ, His only, begotten and eternal Son.

The War of the Ages

"The war of the ages" is real, and it rages on and on.
The battle started in heaven around God's throne.
It began with Lucifer, a beautiful and perfect created being,
who rebelled against God because of his jealousy and envying.
He questioned God's position, authority, laws, and actions.
With the angels, he sowed seeds of doubt and dissatisfaction,
he wanted to begin his own government and replace God's.
His would be better, more fair, and more flexible than the Lord's.

This rebellious and disastrous course God had to bring to an end.
So Lucifer and his angels were cast out of heaven for their sin.
They blamed God for everything, so Lucifer plotted to deceive Eve.
God's sovereignty and loving character, he did not want her to believe.
Eve yielded to his temptation and encouraged Adam to do the same.
Now, both had to leave their beautiful Eden home and take the blame.
Their sin caused the downfall of all mankind forever on this planet Earth.
The only cure is to receive Jesus as Savior and have a new birth.

Today's Changing World

Today, TV soaps like "Bold and Beautiful" never end.
Today, there is too much exposing of the body's skin.
In this world the "bad guys" seem to always win.
In other words, there is too much sin, S-I-N!

The process of destroying hope and love is sin.
Sin destroys families and nations, our faith and trust.
Sin fosters and fuels too much hate, greed, and lust.
S-I-N is a growing cancer, and it must not win!

The nature of mankind is to take all they can.
Self-interest, greed, and lust is what they demand.
Too many prefer to take the evil stand,
and dare anyone to correct or reprimand.

In today's world people think the laws of God are strange.
Many think legislative laws will make the needed change.
Good morals, coming from a pure heart, is what we need.
We must repent of our sins, study God's Word, and let Him lead.

Carnal-Minded People (The Christian Dilemma)

Sometimes it's very difficult
to deal with carnal-minded people.
They often communicate with insults
and misinterpret good and valued results.

Sometimes, when all is very serene,
the carnal-minded cannot stand the peace.
They start a rumor, a grumble, or a scene;
any kind of disturbance that will not cease.

For no particular reason at all,
the carnal-minded is apt to lie or stall.
They practice it every day with skill,
To help misinterpret things that are real.

Christians must watch and pray
about living with the carnal-minded each day.
In God's grace, they must always stay;
while doing His will and showing others the way.

IV. Getting Ready

Much time is spent daily getting ready for various tasks, such as the job, school, going to visit someone, etc.

However, too many people do not get ready for death, which is natural and inevitable. Many are afraid of death and do not understand it.

The poems in this section are written to shed some light on the inevitability of death. My hope is to share some inspiration and understanding for the bereaved.

Are We Ready for Jesus to Return?

People know that Christ is returning to earth again.
Yet, are we living with this fact in mind?
Are we telling others why Christ was slain?
Are we spreading His good news to all mankind?

Do we understand that Jesus' coming is very near?
Just look at the earth, the sky, and the hearts of men.
The predicted "end time" signs are visible and clear!
Yet, most people still deny that the cause is SIN.

We must cast away all sin, every weight and all fears.
We must wholly depend on Christ Jesus alone.
He is the only one who can wipe away all our tears.
He is the only one preparing for us a better home.

There is no more time for godlessness or greed.
He wants us to love, to share, to help, and care
for others who are in physical and spiritual need.
As we seek to do His will, He'll always be there.

He'll be with us to strengthen, lead and guide.
He'll help us travel the lonesome, narrow, and straight way.
We must pray always, study His Word, and in Christ abide,
while we patiently wait for Him to return some day.

Ready to Go Home

Why do relatives moan and are so distraught,
when their loved ones pass away?
Is it because of the loss of a dearly beloved?
Are some things done at their death all for naught?

Why won't we let loved ones depart in peace?
Why do we put them through all the misery
of tubes and machines before they decease?
Is it selfishness, or do we not understand or see?

For the critically ill, death is welcomed and a fact of life.
The Bible says death is only like a deep sleep,
In death, there will be no more tears, pain or strife.
It's a time of rest while we wait for Jesus Christ.

The Understanding

While visiting the hospital, I saw a friend in sorrow.
Her head was drooped and her eyes teary.
I asked, "What is the matter, dearie?
She said, My grandma won't be here long.
She is fading fast and may be gone by tomorrow.

"How old is she," I asked.
"Ninety-five," she replied.
I smiled as I stood by her side.
Saying, "It's a blessing to live that long
and complete so many varied tasks."

I said, "Do you know, my friend,
that she is more than ready to pass on.
This world is not her everlasting home.
She will be resting and waiting for a better place
Where peace, love and happiness never end.

When I left the hospital that day,
my friend had a smile and new outlook.
I am sure her sorrow was not gone.
But she could take her grandma's
passing in a new and less grieved way.

I Am Committed

I am committed to Jesus Christ our Lord,
and I know He wants us to be in one accord.
All the truths I've learned, I can share
with continuous study and lots of prayer.

So, when I give you a little gift of love,
It's because I'm committed to our Lord above.
With your help, changes can be made by the Lord,
because truth is like a two-edged sword.

Do you know, Jesus wants none to be lost?
To save us all, He paid the greatest cost.
He commissioned me to "Go and Tell" each soul,
The Lord is with us, and He is always in control.

This Is My Mission

(Can be sung to the tune of "Blessed Assurance")

Blessed with His goodness, blessed with His love;
Blessed with His showers that come from above.
Blessed with His sunshine, blessed with His air,
I'll go on helping everywhere.

God gives the courage, faith leads the way.
Onward we travel, happy each day.
Thinking of others, willing to share.
Taking God's message everywhere.

God gives the courage, faith leads the way

Remembering others, whenever I pray.
Looking to Jesus, He is the way.
Onward I travel, He's by my side,
Never to falter, He is my guide.

Chorus: This is my mission, this is my prayer,
Helping the needy, everywhere.
This is my mission, this is my prayer,
Helping the needy, everywhere.

V. Patriotism

In the United States of America, patriotism is very pronounced and often very visible, especially during national holidays, and often at sports games. The love for our country is real, and its history is a great history, well-preserved, and known by all.

However, there are many problems in our country. There is a part of the United States that many do not see or know about. A lot of the negative and unpleasant things that affect the population is misunderstood, rationalized, and even ignored. The larger part of the population falls into a category that many of my poems address. This group includes the so-called middle-class, the poor, and their cries for relief.

Where Is the American Dream?

Leaders and professors procrastinate,
Politicians and businessmen manipulate.
Analysts and economists speculate
about the "American Dream."

Leaders and supervisors deliberate
about which workers to eliminate.
Machinery never gets an update,
while all seek the "American Dream."

Writers see our problems and fictionalize.
Leaders see our problems and analyze.
We see our problems and moralize.
For we have "No American Dream."

As problems abound, all want to investigate,
The interest groups just opinionate.
The average working man becomes disconsolate.
He has, nor sees an "American Dream."

Heed the Signs I

Twenty thousand dollars or a little bit more
is paid per year to a family of four.
Workers are laid off by the score.
    HEED THE SIGNS!

Foreign investments are now to an extreme.
Nobody is listening to the workers' scream.
Too many have lost the "American Dream."
    HEED THE SIGNS!

In every town and city, crimes abound.
Law enforcers are often not around.
The leaders say their hands are bound.
    HEED THE SIGNS!

Homelessness is steadily increasing.
All age groups are steadily decreasing.
More pollution the environment is releasing.
    HEED THE SIGNS!

The Desirable Switch

If hard-working people, the backbone of this country,
were paid like professional sports players or actors and such.
If their efforts, contributions, and education were valued just as much,
then let their value be compensated with big bucks!
It would be fantastic to switch and see!

If players earned money like you and I,
the nurses, teachers, policemen, and so many others;
If thousands of dollars were paid per week to us, oh my!
Imagine how different people would value one another.
Wouldn't it be grand to switch and see?

It seems to me that everything is upside down.
The service workers, farmers, builders, and so many more
are the hardest working people in any town.
Think, maybe there would be less homelessness and poor.
It would be a miracle to switch salaries and see!

Tax-Paying Poor

We, the forgotten, the newly unemployed, the homeless,
are making this earnest and sincere plea
to our president, the congress, and leaders we elect.
Please open your hearts, minds, and your eyes to see
that we are the important ones you should protect.
WE, the tax-paying poor of the USA are many.
WE do the work, and expect you to consider us all.
WE are the true power in this depressed and inflated economy.
Without our help the United States is destined for a great fall!

WE say, no more high taxes, no more waste;
no more special interest groups or favoritism;
no more business as usual, no more cynicism!
You have only a short time to demonstrate
that constructed changes are taking place.
Where will you concentrate your efforts, what will you do?
What legislative laws or special groups will you embrace?
Will you remember that WE, the "TAX-PAYING POOR"
are a major part of this great United States too?

Why?

Why is **honesty** quickly discarded
and dishonesty favorably regarded?

Why is **integrity** considered a dirty word,
and those without it are first to be heard?

Why are **good things** given little reviews,
and dirt on anyone or anything gets priority news?

Why is **justice** only swift and sure
for the rich and not the poor?

Why are our hard-earned **dollars and cents**
spent on policies and things that make no sense?

Why … Why … Why …?
I will continue to ask until I die.
Why … Why … Why, I pray.
This is definitely not God's way!

Heed the Signs II

Babies are dying, children are crying,
Politicians seem unconcerned while lying.
Those who are concerned are only sighing,
    HEED THE SIGNS!

The stock market fluctuates up and down.
Foreign politicians are steadily in town.
There's not enough money to go around.
    HEED THE SIGNS!

Changes are experienced every day,
around the world and in the USA.
The same old "gridlock" cannot stay.
    HEED THE SIGNS!

New leaders will be elected.
This time many women were selected.
This is not what the "old cronies" expected.
    HEED THE SIGNS!

A Change Is Needed

A change in this country is definitely needed.
Will the newly-elected leaders heed it?
The people are exclaiming their disgust
of the leaders' greed, dishonesty, and lust!

We, the USA, once soared to the skies.
Today, the USA operates under so many lies.
"In God We Trust" was once proclaimed.
Has this been discarded for riches and fame?

The constant increased taxing of our meager funds
has to **stop** and a better tax system begun.
Taxes are taken from our income and more as we spend.
Then more is taken for something else, again and again!

The needs of all the people must be addressed,
if this country is to continually progress.
Giving our jobs to other countries and their subjects
could be the death of this great and free republic!

Lord, Help Us Through

(A Sincere Prayer for 1992–2022)

All of the necessities of life cannot be paid.
Any unusual expenses of any kind must be delayed.
If this continues, what will the hard-working people do?
Lord, Please help us through … 1992!

This is all the time without any relief foreseen.
It does not matter how much we keep our budget lean.
The bills and taxes will keep coming until we die.
Lord, have mercy! Please let the UNUSUAL pass us by!

The elected officials are so secure and unconcerned.
They have no knowledge of what we really earn.
Our meager salaries of $20,000 or a bit more won't do!
Lord, please help us through … 2002!

What do politicians know when WE pay their way?
Every need is taken care of each and every day.
WE pay for "write-offs," their failures and waste,
their entertainment, travel, and even their bad taste.

There are many answers and avenues for relief.
But they won't be pursued nor compelled
if they cause the so-called upper-class any kind of grief.
Lord, Please help us through … 2012.

Higher wages or better benefits, they say, they can't pay.
So the "poor" get poorer, and things continue in the same way.
While the rich get richer, and waste much of their plenty,
Lord, what can we do to change it all by 2020?

Lord, please help our leaders with your grace.
Please help us to elect the best ones in this 2020 race.
Please show them that **Your rules** and **Your laws**
are the foundation for everything, every group, and every cause.

Everything in the USA will only get worse as time goes by.
Today's beliefs and actions, should make every person try
to improve what has been legislated with a determination to do.
Lord, Lord! Please help us to carry on through 2022!

VI. Unique and Special People

All over the world, there are unique and special people who are not recognized as special. People like mom and dad, the dying grandmother, a baby, boys and girls, the little old man sitting on a bench each day, and so many more.

My poems recognize just a few of the unique people who have crossed my path over the years. Some were very special people.

Your Smile

You have a nice, warm smile
that I simply adore.
You are like a ray of sunshine,
as you come and go.

Tell me all about what you do;
your likes and dislikes too.
What makes you happy or sad;
what makes you anxious or mad.

Your smile can change a negative attitude.
Also, it can show your sincere gratitude.
So, keep smiling as you come and go.
It will become contagious to everyone you know.

keep smiling as you come and go

The Precious Gift

A gem, a jewel, a diamond in the raw;
a precious, unique, and interesting phenomenon;
the phenotype of both dad and mom,
Is the B-A-B-Y.

Then, sleepless nights, feedings, changing
diapers, and walking the floor;
this can't last forever, I am sure.
Right, B-A-B-Y?

Always demanding with expanding lungs,
so time-consuming, no time for fun;
another day has gone, and chores aren't done,
because of the B-A-B-Y.

Is it worth it all? Oh YES, YES!
Will I go through all this again? Maybe.
It is such a unique experience for me,
raising the B-A-B-Y.

Thanks, Mom and Dad

Thank you, Mom and Dad, for all the love, care, and the varied experiences and lessons you have given me. When I needed you, you were always available with whatever help I needed.
    THANK YOU!

You taught me and loved me with a wisdom that comes from God only. You have given me the most valuable education I could ever learn: how to love God and others unselfishly.
    THANK YOU!

You both are so precious to me. I can never express how much I love you and how much I appreciate your gentle, kind and loving ways. I can never repay your unselfish efforts of love.
    THANK YOU!

(Both are sleeping, waiting to go home: Dad in 1995 and Mom in 2007)

Little Black Boy

Little Black Boy ...
You are so confident, bright, and strong.
Little Black Prince ...
You live in a society that treats you so wrong.
Your strength and manhood may be taken.
Your confidence and spirit may be shaken.

Little Black Boy ...
Do not roam the streets to rob, steal, and kill.
Little Black Prince ...
You are here through God's created will.
You are the descendant of noble kings and queens.
You are here to fulfill many great dreams.

Little Black Boy ...
Study! Your grades are too poor.
Little Black Prince ...
Strive for great things; you can do so much more!
You have the power and the key that unlocks
all the doors that are your stumbling blocks.

Old Man

Old man, old man
with the great big smile;
Old man, old man,
you have such a gentle, loving style.

The old man, old man,
appreciates you taking the time
to chat with him for a while.

Mentors

All mentors are very special people.
They have such a warm and caring heart.
They cherish a job well-done,
time well-spent, and doing their part.

Mentors are special and unique people.
They can see needs that others neglect.
They give of themselves willingly and
unselfishly, while teaching others respect.

The Brightest Star in the Galaxy

Sometimes an entire celestial galaxy
cannot be clearly seen because of all
the dust particles and large debris
that block their beaming call.
But, keep on looking.

Some galaxies' stars are so bright.
They stand alone in their brilliance.
They sparkle grandly through the night
with a determined, bright resilience.
So, keep on sparkling!

Some of the stars seem very small.
They do not shine so bright.
But they have a steady glow for all
that shines, unwavering, each night.
So, keep on shining!

This is the way it is with many people.
Some shine bright all the time
with a steady glow of independence.
Others have a low beam but a secure shine.
So, keep on beaming!

When all your skills and talents begin to glow,
such pride and joy to others they will bring.
As your progress is followed, some already know
That you can become a queen or a king.
Just keep progressing!

Some people work hard to reach their goal.
They shine and shine wherever they are.
Some reach great heights untold,
and some become the brightest shining star.
Just keep shining and shining!

Girl

You can call me "Girl" if you like.
Then I can start calling you Joe or Mack.
Calling me "Girl" is not a compliment for sure.
It is not natural, endearing, nor is it pure.
Using "Girl" instead of my name is forced verse
that is not natural, but often rehearsed.

Some women like to be called "Girl"
because it makes their heads swirl.
For those who are a senior, or a little "over the hill"
to be addressed as "Girl" is as good as a pill!
But remember this, and always know,
addressing women as "Girl" is all for show.

Women of God

Through the ages, women helped to spread God's message to others.
They lived pure lives, gave their service, and helped one another.
These were women of all ages, like your mother, and even you.
They were taught by grandmothers, other relatives, and neighbors too.

A few will be mentioned, such as **Anna**, a young widow and prophetess;
And **Ruth**, **Naomi's daughter-in-law**, who was a Moabitess.
There were others who have paved a righteous road,
Like **Dorcas**, the disciple whose life apostle Peter restored.

There was **Deborah**, a prophetess and woman judge of Israel;
Also **Queen Esther**, who saved her people, causing Haman's plan to fail.
There is one more from the Bible, I must surely record,
Mary, the chosen virgin mother of Jesus Christ, our Lord.

Fashion Analysis

I often observe and smile whenever I see
a fashion that's very odd or oddly unique.
Some may refer to them as queer or quaint,
but I consider them totally "fashion free."

I've seen high-top boots that buckle at the top,
worn with a sleeveless floral dress with a tie in the back.
On the person's head was an old "Captain Cook" hat
with a blue peacock feather that had one red dot.

She had a bright, multi-colored purse at the waist,
which was held tightly as she walked in great haste.
I turned to look and see what made so many people stop.
It was her unique, "fashion free" outfit, and it said a lot!

Body Parts Chitchat

While looking in the mirror, a part of **the brain** conveyed,
"You are so cute and charming today, I like how you're arrayed!
I really dig your black, polka-dot, silk shirt
and those three-inch heels and short, tight, leather skirt.

The **waist** said; "Cute, charming?" Please give me a break!
I'm rubbed and squeezed with each movement you make.
The skirt is so tight, I can't breathe, there's no room for air!
I can breathe much better without all this fuss and fanfare."

The **thighs and legs** replied with pain, "A little tightness, be real!
Please ease the strain on my muscles with those high heels!
Also, I need some coverage and warmth in this cold weather.
I'll be more pleased with a long, flare skirt made of leather."

The **knees** chimed, "You think you have some strong points?
Well, I've got strain, coldness, and pain in my joints!
I don't know how much more of this I can take.
These scantily-clad fashions cause me major aches."

The **BRAIN** quickly replied, "All messages have been conveyed.
The beauty, the fashion, and the fad of how she is arrayed
cannot override the message of misery and pain.
I've been sending messages continuously! I'll try again!

VII. God's Little Creatures

I have two very interesting poems about God's little creatures. Both are true stories.

When you take the time to look and listen to the small animals, you can be amused as well as learn a lot about them.

The Transit Bus Hijack

Let me tell you a documented, true story
about a New York City bus hijack.
No one can claim fame or glory
from the natural, unaltered facts.

It was HOT, and everything was not fine,
while the tired people pouted and perked.
They were upset because the bus wasn't on time,
and the air conditioner didn't work!

Steaming hot, the crowded bus traveled along,
not aware of what was happening in the back.
Without any warning, everything went wrong.
"Good grief!" The bus was being hijacked!

The driver looked back to investigate,
and saw passengers screaming and rambling!
He hastily stopped the bus to evacuate,
when he saw a swarm of cockroaches scrambling!

The critters were crawling and flying everywhere.
on the people, the walls, the floor, and the seats.
The roaches were scuffling from the heated motor for air,
and successfully hijacked the bus without defeat!

The Stalking Squirrel

One day across campus I was walking,
when I saw the shadow of something stalking.
I paused for a moment, then quickly looked back
to find a squirrel following my every track.

He walked when I walked and stopped when I did.
His actions reminded me of a playful little kid.
Suddenly I walked faster, his actions to test.
That squirrel did the same when I paused to rest.

He walked when I walked and stopped when I did

When I suddenly stopped, he did too,
as if to say, ha, ha, I'm imitating you.
When we came near his favorite old oak tree,
He scurried up to a limb and stared down at me.

VIII. Mystifying English

ABCDEFGHIJKLMNOPQRSTUVWXYZ

The English alphabets are a puzzle to tots, even though they can understand many words and statements before they are one year old.

Associating words that are spoken with the correct alphabet letters is an intimidating task for small children. With the help of parents and siblings, tots begin the journey of association. Later, school continues the task.

A Tot's Puzzling Journey

To me, letters are a puzzle, all in a row.
A few of them, I think I know.
A is for apple; I saw that in a book.
B is for baby; you should see how ours look!
C is for cat; I stepped on his tail, and he did a loud meow!
D is for Daddy; I'll grow as tall as he is somehow.
E is for eat; I do it morning, noon, and night.
F is for fruit; I had some with my friend Mike.
G is for good; that's what Mommy wants me to be.
H is for horse; they are beautiful and free.
I is for ice cream; I can eat it all day!
M is for Mommy who takes us to the park to play.
Mommy says these are letters, they're everywhere!
They're on all kind of things, even up there.

The Quaint "Q"

"Q" is the seventeenth letter of the alphabet.
It's the first letter of words like **quack**, **quick,** or **quote**.
Other familiar words are **quarter**, **quake,** or **quartet**.
There are many other "Q" words to learn, if you take note.

"Q" words can be lots of fun to say also.
Note how you say **quarter** or **quiver**.
Note how you say **quatrain** or **quiz**.
You can **question** anything you don't know.

The "Q" words can help or **quell** your fear.
Others can send you on a **quest** for knowledge.
Many can help you with things that are **queer**.
All can **qualify** you for something big, like college.

So, always remember the dreaded letter "Q"
Use it to help you bake **quick-bread** for dinner.
Maybe you prefer **quiche** for Sunday breakfast.
Whenever you use the letter "Q," you become a winner.

The Transit "T"

"T" is the twentieth letter of the alphabet.
It represents preciseness or exactness.
"T" begins and is part of a variety of words you can test.
There are many words with a "T" that you have not met.

Many "T" words begin with the **prefix** *trans*,
which means: on the other side of, beyond, or across.
In each of these words, the **prefix** is the boss
and the rest of the word follows its command.

Trans changes a word like **border** to trans-border,
which means: on the frontier line or beyond the frontier line.
In every word example, *trans* will clearly define,
the word, if you keep the parts in proper order.

With the "T," you can **traipse** across the countryside.
You can **travel** to many beautiful places.
You can **toot** your horn at your favorite, familiar faces.
And you can **tread** the **tropics** with **tremendous** pride.

The "T" Trail

The man may traipse or travel to town before noon,
or take time to talk to the old timid tycoon.
He may tarry and play tag on a field of rough turf.
Then he can take a taxicab through bad traffic for a slurp.
While there, he may talk with the technocrat, named McSweela,
while they enjoy a lunch of tempura with tortilla.

As you travel the "T" trail, circle every "T" word.
You may see a word that you have never heard.
All can be found in the dictionary, if you look hard.
Those with a perfect score will get a nice reward.
Learning can be rewarding and lots of fun.
You will understand better after you've begun.

The Unique "U"

The **"U"** is the twenty-first letter of the alphabet.
It is the fifth vowel and is used twice in the word *uranium*.
It has prefixes like "**un,**" "**ultra,**" "**up,**" and "**ur,**"
the beginning of many words you have already met.

Many words are changed with a simple "un,"
such as equal to unequal, like to unlike, saved
to unsaved, and many more to find just for fun.
The list is very long, if you choose to be brave.

I like the "ultra" words that means: "to go beyond."
There is sonic or "ultrasonic," violet or "ultraviolet,"
virus or "ultra-virus," sound or "ultrasound."
Such words go beyond and form an impressive bond.

There are abbreviations that begin with the "U."
Some are "UN," "UPS," "USA," or "UFO."
You can be sure there are many more.
All "U" abbreviation can be quite impressive too.

The Zesty "Z"

"Z" is the twenty-sixth letter of the alphabet.
It has words you know like "zoo," "zebra," and "zap."
But do you know about "zoysia," the wiry grass?
Can you count from "zilch" to a "zillion" yet?

"Z" words can be a lot of fun.
You can skip to the beat of a "zither."
You can be "zany" or act like a "zombie."
Then you can dance like the "zephyr" in the sun.

You can grow and study with "zest."
Then learn about "zymurgy," "zymology," or "zoology."
You may want to learn all about "zirconium,"
or how "zoo spores" affect the desert West.

Whatever you do, don't forget the "Z."
Your child's name can begin with it;
"Zarie," "Zon," "Zonzell," "Zecca," or "Zambarette."
They'll be different from the names given to you and me.

Which Tense Makes Sense?

When do you *sink*, and when do you *sank*?
I have trouble discerning the right tense.
Did the man *drink* or did the man *drank*
until he was *drunk* and talking nonsense.

You must remember the word that represents
the tense in which you "parlay."
He *ran* to the beach is in the past tense,
because he didn't return right away.

I *began* to play before the rain started.
After the shower all the players departed.
I *will begin* again when the rain *has gone*,
unless I decide *to go* back home.

The tenses are not bad if you can remember,
which is the present, past, or future member.
My friend *will come* to visit in May.
Well, she *came* and prepared to stay!

TEACH Services, Inc.
P U B L I S H I N G

We invite you to view the complete
selection of titles we publish at:
www.TEACHServices.com

We encourage you to write us
with your thoughts about this,
or any other book we publish at:
info@TEACHServices.com

TEACH Services' titles may be purchased in
bulk quantities for educational, fund-raising,
business, or promotional use.
bulksales@TEACHServices.com

Finally, if you are interested in seeing
your own book in print, please contact us at:
publishing@TEACHServices.com
We are happy to review your manuscript at no charge.

www.ingramcontent.com/pod-product-compliance
Lightning Source LLC
Chambersburg PA
CBHW042136160426
43200CB00019B/2957